THE COMPLETE
ORCHESTRAL REPERTOIRE SERIES

by RAYNOR CARROLL
Principal Percussion - Los Angeles Philharm

ORCHESTRAL REPERTOIRE FOR THE **GLOCKENSPIEL**, VOLUME I (BT-
Debussy: La Mer, Delibes: Indian Bell Song, Mahler: Symphony No. 4, Moza.... ..wgic Flute,
Prokofiev: Alexander Nevsky, Piano Concerto No. 1, Ravel: Daphnis and Chloé, Respighi: Pines of Rome,
Rimsky-Korsakov: Russian Easter Overture, Saint-Saëns: The Carnival of the Animals, R. Strauss: Also Sprach Zarathustra,
ravinsky: Pétrouchka (1911), Tchaikovsky: The Sleeping Beauty, Wagner: Forest Murmurs, Wotan's Farewell and Magic Fire Music.

ORCHESTRAL REPERTOIRE FOR THE **GLOCKENSPIEL**, VOLUME II (BT-2502 58 pages) **$14.95**
Dukas: The Sorcerer's Apprentice, Glazounov: Violin Concerto, Kodály: Háry János, Mahler: Symphony No. 5,
Ponchielli: Dance of the Hours, Prokofiev: Romeo and Juliet, Scythian Suite, Rachmaninov: Symphony No. 2,
Ravel: Mother Goose, Respighi: Fountains of Rome, Scriabin: The Poem of Ecstasy, R. Strauss: Don Juan,
Tchaikovsky: Capriccio Italien, The Nutcracker, Wagner: Dance of the Apprentices, Siegfried's Rhine Journey.

ORCHESTRAL REPERTOIRE FOR THE **SNARE DRUM** (BT-2503 110 pages) **$17.95**
Bartók: Concerto for Orchestra, Bloch: Schelomo, Borodin: Polovetsian Dances, Debussy: Nocturnes, Kodály: Háry János,
Nielsen: Concerto for Clarinet, Symphony No. 5, Prokofiev: Lieutenant Kijé, Peter and the Wolf, Symphony No. 5,
Ravel: Alborada del Gracioso, Bolero, Daphnis and Chloé, Rapsodie Espagnol, Rimsky-Korsakov: Capriccio Espagnol,
Scheherazade, Rossini: La Gazza Ladra Overture, Schuman: New England Triptych, Symphony No. 3,
Shostakovich: Festive Overture, Symphony No. 7, Symphony No. 10, Sousa: The Stars and Stripes Forever,
J. Strauss: Emperor Waltzes, Stravinsky: Pétrouchka (1911 & 1947).

ORCHESTRAL REPERTOIRE FOR **BASS DRUM** AND **CYMBALS** (BT-2504 82 pages) **$14.95**
Berlioz: Roman Carnival Overture, Symphonie Fantastique, Bizet: Carmen, Debussy: La Mer, Dvorák: Carnival Overture,
Enesco: Rumanian Rhapsody No. 1, Mahler: Symphony No. 1, Symphony No. 3, Mussorgsky: A Night On Bald Mountain,
Prokofiev: Violin Concerto No. 2, Rachmaninov: Piano Concerto No. 2, Rimsky-Korsakov: Capriccio Espagnol, Scheherazade,
Rossini: William Tell Overture, Sibelius: Finlandia, Stravinsky: Pétrouchka (1911 & 1947), The Rite of Spring,
Tchaikovsky: The Nutcracker, Romeo and Juliet, Symphony No. 4.

ORCHESTRAL REPERTOIRE FOR THE **XYLOPHONE**, VOLUME I (BT-2505 64 pages) **$16.95**
Barber: Medea's Meditation and Dance of Vengeance, Britten: The Young Person's Guide to the Orchestra,
Copland: Hoe-Down, Hindemith: Kammermusik No. 1, Holst: The Planets, Kabalevsky: The Comedians,
Messiaen: Exotic Birds, Prokofiev: Scythian Suite, Saint-Saëns: Danse Macabre, Schuman: Symphony No. 3,
Shostakovich: Symphony No. 5, Stravinsky: Firebird (original), Firebird Suite (1919), Pétrouchka (1911 & 1947).

ORCHESTRAL REPERTOIRE FOR THE **XYLOPHONE**, VOLUME II (BT-2506 64 pages) **$16.95**
Bartók: Music for Strings, Percussion and Celesta, Copland: Appalachian Spring, Hayman: "Pops" Hoe-Down,
Kabalevsky: Colas Breugnon Overture, Kodály: Háry János, Prokofiev: Alexander Nevsky, Ravel: Mother Goose,
Revueltas: Sensemayá, Saint-Saëns: The Carnival of the Animals, Shostakovich: Cello Concerto No. 2,
Violin Concerto No. 1, The Golden Age, R. Strauss: Salome's Dance, Stravinsky: Les Noces.

ORCHESTRAL REPERTOIRE FOR **TAMBOURINE, TRIANGLE** AND **CASTANETS** (BT-2507 126 pages) **$16.95**
Berlioz: Roman Carnival Overture, Bizet: Carmen, Borodin: Polovetsian Dances, Brahms: Symphony No. 4,
Britten: Four Sea Interludes, Chabrier: España, Debussy: Iberia, Dvorák: Carnival Overture, Slavonic Dances (opus 46 & 72),
Symphony No. 9, Grieg: Peer Gynt, Liszt: Piano Concerto No. 1, Prokofiev: Piano Concerto No. 3, Ravel: Alborada del Gracioso,
Daphnis and Chloé, Rapsodie Espagnol, Respighi: Pines of Rome, Rimsky-Korsakov: Capriccio Espagnol, Scheherazade,
Rossini: William Tell Overture, Saint-Saëns: Danse Bacchanale, Smetana: The Moldau,
Stravinsky: Pétrouchka (1911 & 1947), Tchaikovsky: Capriccio Italien, The Nutcracker, Symphony No. 4,
Wagner: Die Meistersinger von Nürnberg Prelude, Tannhäuser Overture and Venusberg Music.

ORCHESTRAL REPERTOIRE
FOR THE
GLOCKENSPIEL
VOLUME I

COMPILED BY

RAYNOR CARROLL

Layout and design by Raynor Carroll.

Music engraving by Raynor Carroll using Finale 3.5 by Coda Music Software.

ORCHESTRAL REPERTOIRE FOR THE GLOCKENSPIEL, VOLUME I
2nd Edition
Printed and published in the United States of America by:

Batterie Music
P.O. Box 90014 C
Pasadena, California 91109 USA
Tel/Fax: (626) 798-7144
E-mail: battmusik@aol.com
www.batteriemusic.com

ISBN 0-9650322-2-1

Table of Contents

Acknowledgements

Thanks to the library staff of the Los Angeles Philharmonic - *Ken Bonebrake, Kazue Asawa McGregor, Steve Biagini* and *Deanna Hull* for their helpful assistance.

Additional thanks to *Ken Bonebrake* for music proofing.

Thanks to *Karin Furuta Gustave* for text proofing.

Thanks to *Boosey & Hawkes, C. F. Peters, T. Presser* and *G. Schirmer* for reprint permission.

And thanks to *God* for all of His blessings.

This book is dedicated to my father,

Osborne Wilson Carroll

Preface

Quite often percussionists in symphony orchestras are expected to play on the *glockenspiel*, parts written for the *keyboard glockenspiel* (an instrument similar to the *celesta*). Such parts include:

Dukas - *The Sorcerer's Apprentice*
Mozart - *The Magic Flute*
Ravel - *Daphnis and Chloé, Mother Goose*

Works such as these have become a part of the orchestral percussionist's standard repertoire.

The *keyboard glockenspiel's* range is typically 4 or 5 octaves, whereas the *glockenspiel's* range is usually 2 1/2 octaves. Therefore, when performing such works the percussionist must transpose all or a portion of the part to fit the range of the *glockenspiel*. Thus, presented in this collection are original and transposed versions of those works which extend out of the standard range. The transposed versions are offered as only one of many possible interpretations of these parts. Also included in this collection are works in which the *glockenspiel* plays a prominent part (Kodàly - *Háry János*, Prokofiev - *Alexander Nevsky*, etc.).

Each work is presented in its entirety as much as is practical. Works with extended periods of rests (opera, ballet, etc.) are abbreviated with *"Tacet"* indications. The original instrument for which the part was written is indicated on each version and includes:

Bells - *English*
Campanella - *Italian*
Campanelli - *Italian*
Campanelli a testièra (with keyboard) - *Italian*
Carillon - *French*
Clochettes - *French*
Glockenspiel - *German*
Glockenspiel mit klaviatur (with keyboard) - *German*
Harmonica (glass or metal) - *English*
Jeu de Timbres - *French*
Jeu de Timbres à clavier (with keyboard) - *French*

The playing range is given for each version. Footnotes indicated with a cross (†) are from the original part. Footnotes indicated with an asterisk (*) are those of this collection.

Every attempt has been made for accuracy of the material contained within. In some instances mistakes in the original parts have been corrected, however, inevitably some errors may still exist.

The works presented in volumes I & II of this collection represent some of the most prominent orchestral parts written for the *glockenspiel* in the symphonic literature. However, this collection, by no means includes all such repertoire. Instead, the intent of this collection is to provide material that :

1) the percussionist will probably incur at an audition and
2) the mallet player (professional or otherwise) will most often be required to perform with a symphony orchestra.

In preparing literature for an audition or performance it is recommended that the player obtain a score and listen to various recordings in addition to learning the given part. The following page offers some ideas and suggestions on practicing.

Practicing

> *Practice does not make perfect. Correct practice makes perfect.*

Have short- and long-term goals in mind. Be focused and patient in working toward your goals. Know beforehand what you intend to accomplish in each practice session.

Never sacrifice the basics. Count and make sure that your rhythm and tempo are steady (with and without a metronome).

Listen to the sound you are producing. Strive to achieve the best sound possible. Make sure that you are using the proper stroke technique and striking the bars in the correct area. Record and listen to yourself regularly. Be very critical and demanding.

Use a mirror to check hand position, stroke technique, mallet height, etc.

Practice on a regular basis. It is much more productive to practice daily for an hour, as opposed to practicing once or twice a week for a few hours.

Allocate your time properly. In each session apportion time to:

- *Warm-up properly.* Begin by playing repetitive exercises such as scale patterns and arpeggios slowly. As you loosen up, gradually increase the tempo. Don't play too fast too soon! It is very important to stay relaxed and to maintain control. Always strive for note accuracy.

- *The lesson plan (etude, excerpt, solo, etc.).* First, get an overall idea of the piece by playing through it slowly (see sight-reading below). Then locate and isolate the difficult passages. Use a metronome to sub-divide the beat; and practice each passage very slowly. Make sure that you are accurately playing the notes, rhythm, dynamics and phrasing in addition to using the correct hand position, stroke technique, sticking, etc. If problems persist, divide the passage into smaller segments and play them even slower. After practicing the passage correctly several times, gradually increase the speed of the metronome until the desired tempo is reached. Be patient, don't play the passage while repeatedly making mistakes. If you do so, you are practicing to make mistakes!

- *Sight-reading.* Before the end of every practice session take the time to read through a piece that is unfamiliar to you. Choose a piece that is neither too difficult nor too easy. Before you begin, carefully check the key signature, time signature, tempo markings, repeats, dynamics, sticking, etc. Find the most difficult passage and set a tempo accordingly. Take your time. Don't try to play the piece too fast. Keep a steady tempo. Once you start, do not stop until you have played through the entire piece. When finished, evaluate yourself. It's all right to go back and play through or practice the piece, but this now becomes practicing and is no longer sight-reading.

> *Keep in mind that the reason you are practicing is not merely to play the notes, but ultimately to make music.*

La Mer

Three Symphonic Essays for Orchestra

C. Debussy
(1862-1918)

No. 1 - *De l'aube à midi sur la mer* : TACET

No. 2 - *Jeux de vagues*

No. 3 - Dialogue du vent et de la mer

Glockenspiel or Célesta

(transposed version)

La Mer
Three Symphonic Essays for Orchestra

C. Debus
(1862-1918

No. 1 - *De l'aube à midi sur la mer* : TACET

No. 2 - *Jeux de vagues*

Play one octave higher if low "F" is not available.

No. 3 - Dialogue du vent et de la mer

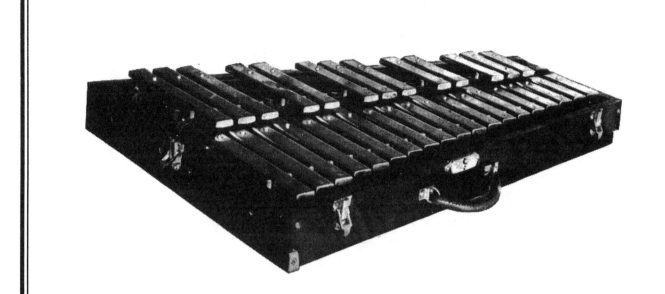

Deagan Parsifal Bells
No. 60

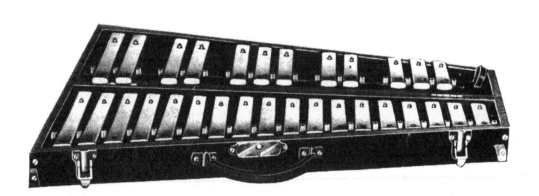

Deagan Roundtop Orchestra Bells
No. 1123

Indian Bell Song
from the Opera

Lakme

L. Delibe
(1836-1891)

Symphony No. 4

G. Mahler
(1860-1911)

III

IV : TACET

†) klingen lassen = let vibrate

Glockenspiel

(original version)

W. A. Moza
(1756-179

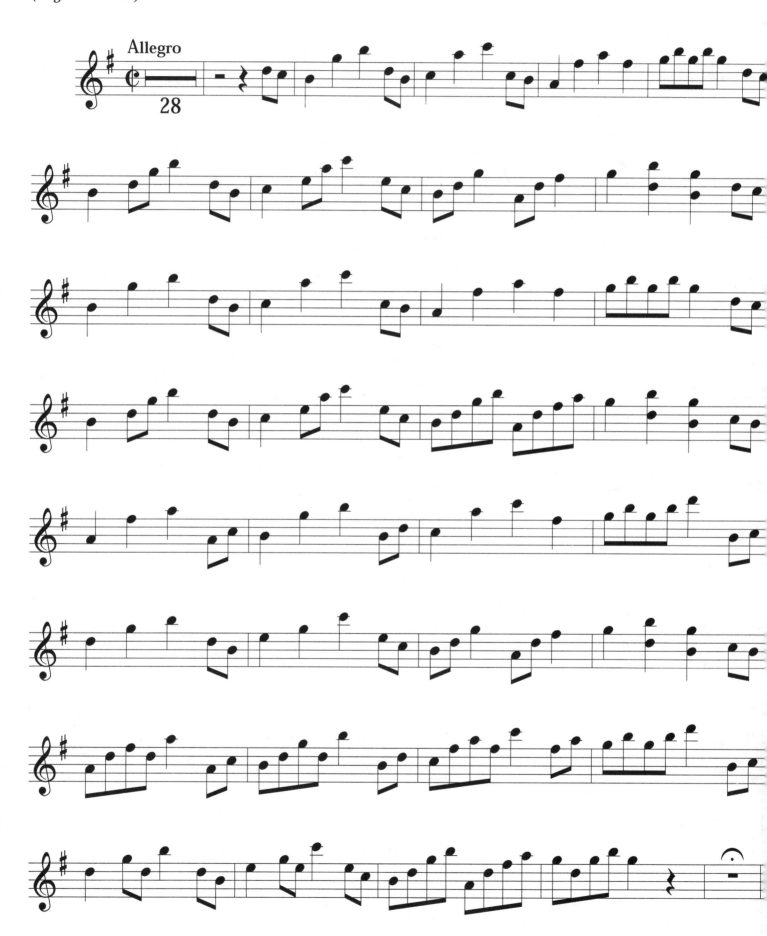

Glockenspiel

(transposed version)

No. 8, Finale
from Act I of the Opera
The Magic Flute

W. A. Mozart
(1756-1791)

Alexander Nevsky

Cantata for Chorus and Orchestra

Campanelli

(original version)

S. Prokofiev
(1891-1952)

No. 1 - 6: TACET

No. 7 - Alexander's Entry Into Pskov

Campanelli

(original version)

Piano Concerto No. 1

S. Prokofiev
(1891-1952)

Campanelli

(2nd transposed version)

Piano Concerto No. 1

S. Prokofiev
(1891-1952)

-26-

Jeu de Timbres

(original version)

Daphnis and Chloé

2nd Suite

M. Ravel
(1875-1937)

Jeu de Timbres

(transposed version)

Daphnis and Chloé
2nd Suite

M. Rave
(1875-1937

Pines of Rome

I. Pines of the Villa Borghese

O. Respighi
(1879-1936)

IL RESTO TACET

Pines of Rome

I. Pines of the Villa Borghese

O. Respighi
(1879-1936)

Campanelli
(transposed version)

IL RESTO TACET

Campanelli

(original version)

Russian Easter Overture

N. Rimsky-Korsakov
(1844-1908)

Russian Easter Overture

Campanelli

(transposed version)

N. Rimsky-Korsako
(1844-190

*) *See footnote on page 39.*

Play one octave higher if low "F" is not available.

The Carnival of the Animals

Introduction, No. 1 - 6 : TACET

No. 7 - Aquarium

C. Saint-Saë
(1835-192

No. 8 - 13 : TACET

No. 14 - Finale

The Carnival of the Animals

Introduction, No. 1 - 6 : TACET

C. Saint-Saër
(1835-1921

No. 7 - Aquarium

*) *Begin on "G" if low "E" and "F" are not available.*

No. 14 : Finale

Glockenspiel

(original version)

Also sprach Zarathustra!

R. Strauss
(1864-1949)

Glockenspiel

(transposed version)

Also sprach Zarathustra!

R. Strauss
(1864-194...)

*) Play one octave higher if low "F#" is not available.

Campanelli

Pétrouchka
(1911)

I. Stravins
(1882-197

(original version)

Pétrouchka
(1911)

I. Stravinsi
(1882-197

Clochettes

(original version)

No. 6, Waltz
from the Ballet
The Sleeping Beauty

P. Tchaikovsky
(1840-189

No. 6, Waltz
from the Ballet
The Sleeping Beauty

P. Tchaikovsky
(1840-1893)

Glockenspiel

(original version)

Forest Murmurs
arranged from the Opera
Siegfried

R. Wagr
(1813-18

*) *Notes added to match the flute (not in original part or score).*

Forest Murmurs
arranged from the Opera
Siegfried

R. Wagner
(1813-1883)

Notes added to match the flute (not in original part or score).

Glockenspiel

(original version)

Wotan's Farewell and Magic Fire Music
from the Opera
Die Walküre

R. Wagi
(1813-18)

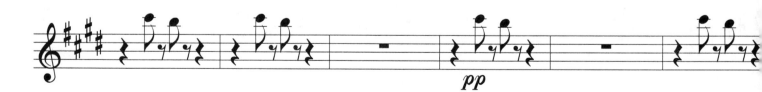

Wotan's Farewell and Magic Fire Music
from the Opera
Die Walküre

R. Wagner
(1813-1883)

Raynor Carroll

has been playing timpani and percussion for the Los Angeles Philharmonic since joining the orchestra in 1983. He has performed under such conductors as Carlo-Maria Giulini, André Previn, Esa-Pekka Salonen, Leonard Bernstein, Pierre Boulez and Zubin Mehta. Mr. Carroll records motion picture soundtracks for Hollywood studio composers including Maurice Jarre, David Newman and Arthur Rubinstein. Mr. Carroll teaches timpani and percussion both privately and at California State University, Los Angeles where he has served on the faculty since 1984.